THAT NEW ENGLAND

Edited by Robb Sagendorph

and Judson D. Hale

FIFTH PRINTING
Library of Congress Catalog
Card Number 66-29385
ISBN 0-911658-55-6

Typeset, Printed, Engraved and
Bound in the United States of America
on paper manufactured in the U.S.A.

FOREWORD

Since 1935, the editors of YANKEE have been collecting photographs, old and new, for use in YANKEE Magazine. As the years have rolled by, a large segment of this collection became one containing photographs of sailing ships, autos, trains, equipment, industries and numerous other scenes—all of which, in their natural form, do not exist today. Were anything to happen to this part of YANKEE's collection (there is always the chance of fire, theft, accidents, carelessness and even decay), many of these photographs would be gone forever. It is better kept, we feel, in a book of this kind—in many places rather than buried here in our files. By enlargement and the careful use of subtle duotone-color printing, we have made every effort to make the reproductions here even more interesting and enjoyable than the originals from which they were taken. The response to the first printing of this book, published in November 1966, was overwhelming. It is gratifying for us to know that the high regard we place on these old photographs is shared by others.

An index and credits appear on pages 190-1. The first draft of this book was made by Robb Sagendorph, founder and publisher of YANKEE. The final draft and layout were done by Judson D. Hale. Esther A. Fitts and Maureen Hayes contributed greatly in the way of research, typing and assistance in layout. C. Robertson Trowbridge was responsible for marketing and promotion plans. However, as YANKEE itself took none of these pictures, but acted only as purchaser and collector, it is only fair to say that whatever honor or praise is due belongs mostly to the photographers who took these old-time pictures. What today is simply the click of a shutter on a tiny "you-do-nothing" camera was, back then, the managing of a huge, heavy contraption on a tripod which used glass negatives and had innumerable adjustments to be made before each picture. And, as 1/30th of a second was considered "fast," unbelievable patience was a prime ingredient.

It is our hope that you will enjoy reading and looking at this book for years to come as much as we have enjoyed the making of it.

Robb Sagendorph
Judson D. Hale

July 15, 1968

Pittsburg, New Hampshire
about 1915

The world's only
7-masted schooner, the
Thomas W. Lawson, as
she was often seen—under
full sail—in Boston
Harbor. She was
the largest all-steel
schooner ever built and
was wrecked on Friday,
December 13, 1907, in a
terrific storm off
Lands End, England. There
were only two survivors.

Who's next?

The first train into Belmont, New Hampshire, on its first run (1887).

Shortly after this photo was published in YANKEE, several conflicting letters were received identifying the team, the date, etc. The following letter, from Daniel Brown of Reading, Mass., seemed to recognize more details than the rest:

"The picture of the fire engine in the December 1965 issue caught my eye and brought back memories. It is very easy to be mistaken and I may possibly be, but I doubt it very much. During the school year of 1919 and 1920 I attended school at Wentworth Institute in Boston. One Sunday there was a fire on Parker Hill. I believe it was Allegany St. which crosses Parker St. just south of Tremont St.—just beyond Roxbury Crossing. The engine with the five horses came up the hill and were almost to the fire when the lead pair reared up, whirled around, and started down the hill on a dead run.

"Four firemen grabbed each horse's bridle and were dragged along to within a hundred feet or so of the fence before the railroad tracks. (A dead end across Parker St.)

"It would seem almost impossible that there would be another rig with two white horses and a black with the engine and a black and white lead pair all in the right location. Also, I remember a white diamond marking on the black horse's face. It would be my bet that that rig was around Roxbury Crossing area not too far away in years from 1920."

The old Sandwich Glass Works, Sandwich, Cape Cod, Mass. No part of
this famous old factory remains standing today. Richard A. Bourne of Hyannis, however,
has quite a large collection of fragments gathered from its
foundation and there are others who still have enough small pieces to mount
them in jewelry. In Sandwich proper is the Sandwich Glass Museum devoted mainly
to Sandwich glass—a most beautiful and valuable display.
At right is a sample of Sandwich glass—decorated by the famous Mary Gregory.

Simonsville, Vermont

The Crowells—R. R., Henry, Preston—and
Herbert Hale—in front of Crowell's Store,
Bernardston, Mass.

The 15-Mile Handicap Race of the Harvard
Bicycle Club on November 18, 1887. The par-
ticipants are (from left to right): Doane, Mark
Richardson, R. D. Herrick, A. E. Burr, Eliot
Norton, R. H. Davis, E. A. Bailey, A. H. Willi-
ams, K. B. F. Hesseltine, T. W. McCansmore,
Codman. (The last two are off the picture).

Lost with All Hands . . .

The side-wheeled steamer *Portland* was lost in the Great Gale of November 26-27, 1898—presumably in a collision with the granite schooner *Addie E. Snow* off Provincetown, Mass.—though no one knows for sure just what actually happened. Of the 190 passengers aboard, all perished. She lies today in 144 feet of water about six miles out to sea from Highland Light.

Lost with All But 19 . . .

At approximately 10:45 on the clear, starlit night of February 11, 1907,
the coal schooner *Harry P. Knowlton* crashed into the port side
of the steamship *Larchmont* as she steamed down the Rhode Island coast with an
estimated 300 passengers and crew. (As with the *Portland*, the passenger
list was lost with the ship). The *Larchmont* went under
in just 12 minutes—with all but 19 passengers losing their lives.

Arriving at the "Yale Bowl" (before there was
a Yale Bowl) in New Haven, Conn.

Calvin and Grace Coolidge received notification in 1920, at the Adams House in Boston, of his nomination by the Republican Convention for Vice President. In order to take this picture (left), Alton Blackington crawled up on the fire escape of the hotel and was let in a window by Mrs. Coolidge —"How foolish you are to be out in this rain without your rubbers," she told him. Mr. Coolidge then loaned him a raincoat. "How do you like the idea of going to Washington?" Blackington asked him, in all the confusion. "Ain't elected yet," was Cal's reply. He also added that "Nobody can mess up a room as quick as a photographer."

Above, three years after he was President, Mr. and Mrs. Coolidge are shown celebrating his 59th birthday at White Court, Swampscott, Mass.—July 4, 1931 —two years before he died.

The start of the America Cup Race,
September 11, 1886.
The American *Mayflower* is on
the left, the British *Galatea* on the
right. The race was won by the
Mayflower. This was the sixth occasion
of this sailing classic—the
first having been held
between Britain's *Aurora*
and America's *America* on August 22, 1851.

MAY FIRST
NINETEEN
HUNDRED
AND TWO

Camden, Maine, from Mount Battie.

Note the schooners in the harbor and bay beyond.

The 5:15 pulling out of the North Station, Boston—the old-time commuters' last chance for a hot dinner at home.

Building the Great Ships...

In the very early days, the ships' carpenters went into the nearby woods and located trees in which the shapes of the needed timbers were contained—see above, left. These trees were then felled and dragged by oxen to the building yard. The above photo shows the *H. W. Macomber* with its frame and ribs all set up. The inside planking is being installed. Great strength was built into this part of the construction as, for reasons of cargo strain, the inside had to be even stronger than the outside.

Building the Great Ships...

The frame pieces were assembled on a platform even with the hull and bolted together before being hoisted into place. Then followed the inner planking or "ceiling," the outer planking—squared and re-squared—and much hand-caulking. The photo in the middle, above, shows the ship *Brown Brothers* at the Atkinson and Filmore Yard, Newburyport in 1875. A pair of oxen appears off to the right of Ben Balch (the high hat usually indicated an "owner").

Building the Great Ships...

(1)

(2)

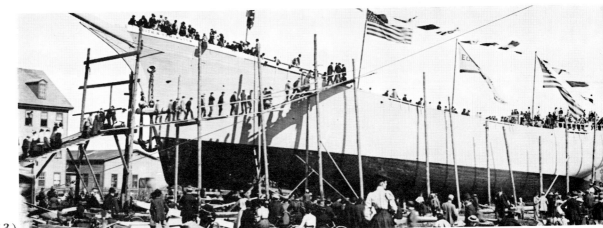

(3)

(4)

(5)

(1) The *Helen J. Seitz*—launched October 31, 1905 at Camden, Maine.
(2) The *Ontario*, 1866. She and her sister ship, the *Erie*, were the largest wooden steamships built on the Merrimac River. (3) The *Edith H. Symington*, built by William S. Currier in 1900. This launching at Newburyport was a great event—178 carriages and 87 boats were on hand.
(4) Launching of the gunboat *Marblehead*—October 16, 1861—on the Merrimac River. (5) The schooner *Geneva*, built in 1900 at Butler-Cobb Yard, Rockland, Maine. She was lost July 13, 1912, off Itaparica, Brazil.

After the Blizzard, Monson,
Mass. You shovelled
out then—before the automated
plows and trucks—or you
were snowed in 'til spring!

Entertaining the horses while the load is being forked

onto the wagon at Biddeford, Maine. Note the man-sized rake.

On the Charles River
near Weston, Mass.

The top photo shows H. B. Sweet of Pittsfield, N. H.—the last old-time "tin peddler" of Maine, New Hampshire, and Vermont. An auctioneer at one time, too, Sweet was said to be one of the men who made the expression "Yankee trading" the byword for shrewdness that it is today.

"I had more friends than a politician," he once recalled as an old man. "I guess I knew most of the storekeepers and farmers' wives in the state. I always spent the night with some friendly farmer. I would eat supper with the family, sit around the fire and talk, and then go to bed. I hardly ever paid cash for my night's lodging, but usually traded a dishpan or a teapot worth about half a dollar for my food and bed. Only once did I ever stop at a hotel. One night about supper time, I was caught between two towns in a terrible thunderstorm. It rained so hard that I had to bore a hole in the bottom of my wagon to let the water run out. Well, I pulled into an inn for supper, and it cost me 60 cents. When I got home, the man I worked for said that was a terrible extravagance and refused to allow the 60 cents on my expense account.

"I used to carry almost everything on that old wagon of mine. We hardly ever used money in those trades—it wasn't necessary. Why, once I traveled for nearly a month with only 13 cents in my pocket. I never got any more or less during the whole trip. I did nearly all my trading for farm products, cloth, and anything that the farmer wanted to trade. You would hardly believe some of the loads I used to pick up. I always managed to sell everything—from sewing needles to silos. One time, a fellow I knew thought that I was getting a little too proud of my ability to drive a bargain. He called me out to his farm one day with the promise that he had something that I wouldn't dare to trade. When I got out there I found that it was an old, wrinkled Merino buck, tough as nails and looking as if most of his wool had been eaten off by moths. I traded him though, and when I got home, I sold the old buck to my father who skinned off the pelt and fed the meat to his hired men!"

The bottom photo is of O. C. Hunn's "Order Wagon," East Longmeadow, Mass.—looks like he traded something or other for a bunch of potted sunflowers.

Dobbin eyes his competition—Westford, Vt. Names on the old glass negative from

which this print was taken include Floyd A. Grow, Weslie Steadman, and Joe **Lamerr.**
The car looks to be a Reo of about 1910 **vintage.**

HUMPHR
CO
STORAGE

OLD COLONY
CREAMERY

Bark C.W.Morgan

CH

The famous whaling bark *Charles W. Morgan* is shown here
in three stages of her life. As a working
whaler—before she was laid up on the beach in concrete
on the estate of Col. E. H. R. Green at South Dartmouth, Mass. Middle: En route to
Mystic Seaport, Conn. Right: At Mystic Seaport—as she appears today.

This page: Miss Wentworth and
Miss Kiff, above, secretaries in
the office of the B. M. Co. in
Bernardston, Mass. and, right,
another old-fashioned stenographer,
unidentified. Opposite page: Old-time draftsmen, top—note
that one gentleman works with
his hat on. Below, another office in the B. M. Co.

The drudgery of "bucking up" cordwood for the yearly fuel supply was an irksome task 60 years ago. One teen-age youth said there were three things he didn't like to do—dig potatoes, saw wood, and work. In the top photo on this page, George Gowing's (Dublin, N.H.) "Old Bill" provides

the horsepower. Bottom photo (opp.) is John Pike and his two-horse rig from Goshen, N.H. Pike went from farm to farm cutting wood. On this page is the "one lunger" gas engine saw which replaced the horse rigs. The old couple lived in Windsor, Vt.

Above: Gathering maple sap at the Cleary Farm in Williamsburg, Mass.—
April 2, 1940. The old gentleman is Arthur Wade (red whiskers and red hair) who
was reputed to be one of the best oxen drivers in the country. While he
carried the familiar whip, he was never known to use it.
He would simply walk ahead of his team and they would
follow. Right: "The Monarch"—Otis Goss Farm in Goshen, Mass.

Barnum & Bailey Circus Parade, New Haven, Connecticut

60

The Pung Ride, Hingham, Massachusetts

Converse Trufant—a Francestown, New Hampshire blacksmith who, in his later years, became a craftsman in decorative ironwork.

F.E. Chandler, blacksmith of Kingston, Mass. Photo was taken April 8, 1929. Tool boxes such as his are sought-after antiques today.

In early days, all up and down the New England coast, salt marsh hay was a valuable crop. Usually harvested during the very low tides of the Harvest Moon, it was stacked up on poles, as shown left, along the Merrimac River near Plum Island. If not before, it would be hauled home on wagons when the marshes were frozen solid. Above, a gundalow is being unloaded near Salisbury. At far left are several gundalows —including one taking a pleasure cruise.

Old-time Lane
Parsonsfield, Maine

Dressed to the hilt for a country joy-ride and cook-out—Vermont (1912).

Robert Frost—at Derry, New
Hampshire (far right) and
Ripton, Vermont.

Roaring through East
Greenwich, Rhode Island, 1934

Waiting for the milk train at Winchester, New Hampshire.

Providing a drink for the cows near Hanover, Massachusetts.

Above, the East Boston Ferry—later replaced by the Callahan and Sumner Tunnels. Shown left, a Boston Harbor pilot boat—used by Cap'n J. K. Lunt and other pilots.

All of these scenes of 19th Century lifesavers were taken at Plum Island. The station shown here housed all the lifesaving equipment. The barrels to the right of the building were used to catch "soft" rain water off the roof. The photo at bottom, right, shows clearly the details of a lifeboat ready for launching. Note the canvas tube running the length of the boat at the rail. This was filled with cork to keep the boat afloat if it filled.

Later boats had a false floor through the bottom of the boat. Water taken in would then run overboard again. A mast with sail was lashed along the seats. During night disasters, the shore was lighted, as shown here, to guide possible survivors. At the turn of the century, the lifesavers were not on duty from July first through October first—it was thought there would not be any wrecks in good summer weather. Later, most stations operated year 'round.

The one-
horse
shay,
Ludlow,
Vermont—
about 1910.

When oxen were in vogue "way back then," they were
used for moving houses (right), and any other jobs
(Spaulding Abbott is the teamster, above right)
which required strength. Sometimes, they were used
for fun—as at the Hayseed Tally-ho, above, at the
old Sinclair House in Bethlehem, New Hampshire.

The vanishing Shakers—Canterbury,
New Hampshire (1954). Without
children or successors, this celibate
sect, founded in 1774, is now about
run out. There were other
colonies at Pittsfield, Massachusetts
and at Sabbathday Lake, Maine.

At the Harvard-Yale boat race, New London, Connecticut

"Ready to Roll"—the
fire horses were
backed under the raised
engine harnesses.

THE LAST DRIVE

■ THE LAST LOG DRIVE ON THE CONNECTICUT RIVER WAS IN 1909. It was the biggest in the long and picturesque career of George Van Dyke who had been in the lumber business for over 50 years. At the age of 11, after four years of schooling, he had begun to shift for himself. He rose from chore boy in a logging camp to head of the powerful Connecticut Valley Lumber Company.

The 1909 drive (at which the accompanying photos were taken) contained 40 million feet of lumber, the largest ever sent down the Connecticut. The rear crew was 60 strong— the cream of an army of 600 men employed in former years. This falling off in the size of the crews did not mean a smaller drive but pointed to a better knowledge of the river and an ability to keep the channels as full of logs as the water would permit. The drive started about April 6th. Each little stream floated its quota of logs into the main river—from Colebrook, Bloomfield, and Granby. There were stirring times in these little brooks while the flood waters lasted. Jams were dynamited since there was no time to pick them apart by man power. When the logs were assembled in the mainstream, the crews were put through the "sifter." That is to say, the bosses of the various sections picked out their best men and the rest were discharged.

Life on the river itself was both colorful and busy. Many old-timers will remember *Mary Ann,* the "wan'gan" a large

(continued on page 92)

90

houseboat on which meals were cooked whenever possible and on which some of the men slept. At the falls, the "wan'gan" was resolved into sections and hauled by six-horse teams to be reassembled later. On occasions like these, men would dig holes in the river bank and fill them with preheated stones and bake beans in crocks covered with hemlock bows. Rafts large enough to float 10 horses were constructed, and the animals practically lived on them except when it was necessary to pass some dam or rapid. There were several "bateaux" with outfits to carry grain and baled hay for the horses, as well as sleeping tents and blanket rolls for the use of the cant-hook crews working on a jam, not to mention the "quick Billy" canoes.

The log driver worked hard. Up at four a.m., he had breakfast and went right to business. At nine in the morning he had luncheon and at two p.m. another meal and, finally, supper at eight in the evening. He worked every day of the week, including Sundays, and was up to his waist in water every minute that he was not in bed. His feet got sore and would eventually put him into the hospital unless he took very good care of them. Most of the old-timers covered their feet with lard or vaseline whenever an opportunity presented itself.

Because of a law requiring the rafting of logs in Massachusetts, and the operations of the Connecticut Valley Lumber Company which embraced the building of a large mill at Barnet, Van Dyke felt that logging on the Connecticut would soon come to an end and that this drive in 1909 would be his last. He little knew how right he was.

On August 7, 1909, Van Dyke was watching his driving crews from a high bluff overlooking the river at Turner's Falls. After giving directions about sluicing the logs, he got into his car and told his chauffeur to drive him farther down the river. The chauffeur put the car into reverse and it plunged over the cliff.

End

The Little Red
    (once red?)
School House in
    Rochester, Vermont—
        and, lower right, Bernardston, Massachusetts

Boyhood's golden days—Parsonsfield, Maine

Woodstock, Vermont. The Eagle Hotel (left) is now the location of the Woodstock Inn.

Hutchinson House (right) is now the White Cupboard Inn.

T Wharf and the Boston Fishing Fleet. Most of the vessels here have their topmasts down as the winter gales on the Banks were too severe for topsails. None of these ships had any power. Note the small "shore haul" schooners on the left of both pictures.

The family portrait, in days of yore,
required not only skill but patience.

When clams were plentiful and fat and clam digging was an industry,
Jack Harris and George Washington Peebles, below, of Newburyport, Massachusetts,
made a good living. That their shanty door is hanging by
one hinge bothers them no more than it does Peebles' contented tiger cat.

Snow rollers such as these in Dublin, New Hampshire
(bottom left) and in Ludlow, Vermont
were used to harden the surface for sleighing.

Ad Butler, known as an "Old 'Squammer,"
at Coffin's Beach on the Annisquam River,
Annisquam, Massachusetts (about 1900).

(1)

(2)

This is an old-fashioned barn raising—somewhere in northern Connecticut before 1900 and recorded by Alvah and George Howes, roving photographers. In photo #1, the men are squaring up the timbers. A man at left holds a beetle for hammering on the chisel. Also in the picture are an adz, broad axe, and handsaw. In photo #2, the men are making mort-

ises and tenons to fit the beams together. The seated men are drilling holes. Photo #3 shows a section or bent being raised into position. In photo #4, the bent is in place and other timbers will be readied for the next section. A few hours later, the ladies will provide a sumptuous meal to be enjoyed by one and all.

Only one hoof . . . . . probably at West Roxbury near Boston

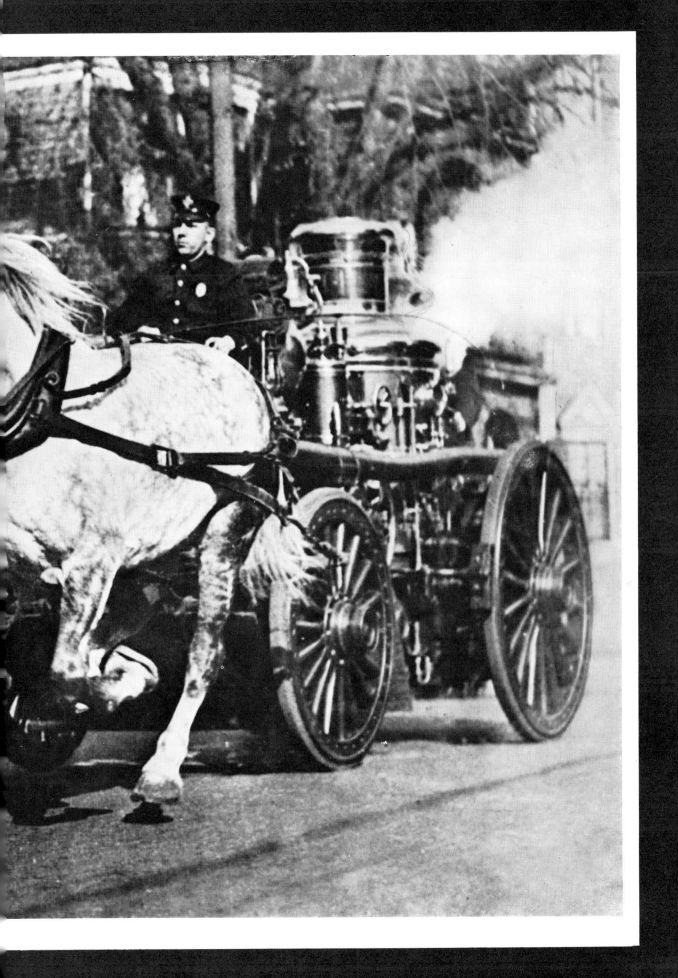

Hill-climbing
contest, 1908, on
Yale Center Hill,
New Haven, Connecticut

In the Spring of 1928, RFD carrier Maxim's Chevrolet had to be rescued by oxen
from the mud. After the rescue, Farmer
Strothers asked him why the mail was late.

The *James Arnold* (1890), America's last full-rigged whaler and, right, the *Kathleen*, the last whaler stove and sunk by a whale. (There were only three such sinkings by whales recorded.)

KATHLEEN OF NEW BEDFORD.

Old-time Connecticut River ferries included the wire ferry at Windsor, Vt., above;
the Hockanum Ferry, shown at top left as it is about to land on the Northampton,
Mass. shore in 1901 (in the background are Mt. Holyoke and part of the town of
Hadley); and the one shown, left, being poled somewhere across the Connecticut.

THE "LOOKS" OF YESTERYEAR...

(1) In the second decade of the 20th Century, the "flapper" craze had the old folks wondering.

(2) Easter bonnets of the 1880s.

(3) To go ice fishing in 1910 at the Country Club in Brookline, Massachusetts, this is what the ladies wore.

(4) The "city look," Boston.

(1)

(2)

(3)

123

L'Estudiantina Waltz

(1)

(2)

The Old Fall River Line
1847-1937

The first whistle of the Fall River Line blew at Fall River in 1847. The occasion was the linking up of a rail-water route between Boston and New York—the rail part of which had been finished in 1845. By 1894, the line had the *Priscilla*—"the greatest steamboat ever known"—in her fleet. In 1906-1907, with the line at its peak, it ran into competition with the old *Harvard* and *Yale*, direct steamers between New York and Boston which ran outside Cape Cod. In 1916, with the opening of the Cape Cod Canal, this competition cut down its run by at least five hours under her "outside-the-Cape" run of 15 hours. After considerable cajolery, ultra-conservatism, etc., among steamship, railroad, and labor magnates (and improved railroad and automobile facilities), the line ceased operation.

Shown here are **(1)** the *Plymouth* (1890) passing under the Mount Hope Bridge for the stop at Newport and then on to New York; **(2)** the *Priscilla* (1894) as it passes under the Bourne Bridge over the Cape Cod Canal on June 17, 1937—the first and last time that the Fall River steamer (side-wheeler) ever went through the Cape Cod Canal; **(3)** the *Commonwealth* leaving the Newport Repair Shops for dry dock at Hoboken, New Jersey—May 15, 1935.

(3)

More Old Steamships...

Volumes could be written about the steamships of New England; the Nantasket-Boston, the New Bedford-Nantasket, the Boston-New York, the Boston-Yarmouth, the Boston-Portland, etc.

Here is the old side-wheeler *Mount Desert* (1). In 1875, she was placed in service on the Rockland Harbor, Maine, run by the Sanford Steamship Company. She operated until 1904.

The old *Dorothy Bradford* (2) ran between Boston and Provincetown, Massachusetts. The *King Philip*, at an adjoining Boston dock, was in use at the time this picture was taken (1930?) for daily fishing trips to the Banks.

Finally, (3) the Nantasket Beach Line's *Rose Standish* taking a holiday excursion for the grand opening of the just-completed Cape Cod Canal in 1916.

(1)

(2)

(3)

8:30 a.m. at East Rock, Connecticut, 1908

IN THE GOOD OLD SUMMERTIME

Top, left: Remember the famous "Rocking Chair Brigades"—those who went to summer hotels and just sat on the veranda and rocked? This is the old Sinclair Hotel in Bethlehem, New Hampshire. Tennis or violin anyone? *Bottom, far left:* the Lighthouse, New Haven, Connecticut, 1908. *Above:* Pancake Picnic. *Near left:* Old Orchard Beach—Pier Ride, 1909.

Wharf scene—New Bedford, Massachusetts, 1870. The
barrels contain whale oil
destined for this country's now-antique "whale oil" lamps.

Civil War veteran Freeman F. Elkins
trims and lights old street lamp near his home
at Weirs, New Hampshire

The "new" acetylene
had to be lit
with a pressure
torch (near Boston)

This lamp, being lighted by Professor
William Monroe, was to guide hikers using the trails on
Camel's Hump Mountain in Vermont

New Hampshire "Mountain Wagon"

Old Stagecoach, Williamstown, Massachusetts.

Bark Josephine Drying Sails

1▲

2▲

3▲

4▲

5▲

6▲

Are No More...

1. Butterfield Bridge, Perkinsville, Vt. 2. Upper Cox Brook Bridge, Northfield, Vt. 3. W. Manchester, N.H., 4. Second bridge over the Mascoma R., the Packard Hill Bridge, E. Lebanon, N.H. 5. E. Lebanon, N.H. 6. Buzzell's Bridge, west of Union Village, Vt. 7. Barre.

1▲

2▲

3▲

4▲

5▲

1. Dingman's Bridge, Weathersfield, Vt. 2. Ledyard Bridge, Hanover, N.H. 3. Rock's Bridge, E. Haverhill-W. Newbury, Mass. 4. Old Bridge at Hancock-Greenfield, N.H. 5. "New" Bridge at Greenfield-Hancock, N.H. 6. Bridge at Foxcroft, Maine (May 8, 1911). 7. Old Republican Bridge, Franklin, N.H.

6 ▲

7 ▲

1 ▲

2 ▲

3 ▲

4 ▲

5 ▲

1. R. R. Bridge, Bennington, N.H. 2. Runnell's Bridge, Hollis Depot, N.H. 3. Londonderry, N.H. 4. Haverhill, N.H. 5. Bridge between Bradford and Haverhill, Mass. 6. Walker Bridge, Grafton, Vt. 7. Bennington, N.H.

6 ▲

7 ▲

147

Winchester, New Hampshire

Somewhere in New England—before 1900

A typical example of the steam launch is the *Gipsy* **(1)**—with the Wentworth Hotel at Newcastle, N.H. in the background (1886). After steam came launches powered by naphtha, keroscne, and gasoline.

The naphtha launch *Ruth-Louise* **(4)** is shown here, probably at the Bluffs near Newburyport. It was owned by Albert Titcomb (lèaning on the awning). In the stern are Mr. and Mrs. Shepard who owned a fine summer resort at Carr's Island. The naphtha launch was extremely prone to fire or explosion.

At Salisbury Point, Mass. in the 1880s, there lived a "ne'er-do-well" named Charles D.

(1)

Mosher. He hated work. In fact, his wife kept boarders to support him while he played the harmonica and dreamed. Well, one of his dreams was a speedboat model which eventually became, with the cooperation of George Manson, the *Buzz* **(2)**. She made 30 miles per hour and was the fastest boat in the world at that time. The *Buzz* (shown here in Boston Harbor) led Mosher to high naval office, and to a private practice in hydraulics.

Mosher also designed the *Arrow* **(3)** for millionaire stockbroker Crane's use on the Hudson. She made 46.5 nautical miles per hour on her trial trip—a record never broken for a boat of her displacement.

(2)

(3)

(4)

At low tide, a whaler could be pulled over on her side by halyards from her masts in order to have her keel and hull repaired. Here is the bark *Josephine* of New Bedford in this embarrassing position. At right is the whaler *Sunbeam* undergoing repairs on her stern. Note the carved eagle—what a valuable antique it would be today!

154

"After the Decoration Day Parade,"
above, and "Home for Thanksgiving"—both
taken in 1897.

Many readers of these pages will remember the electric trolley car—both closed and open. Present-day readers, however, will not have ridden behind the horse or donkey-engine trolleys which existed before the electric trolleys came along in the 1880-90s. Both horse-drawn **(1)** and donkey-engine-drawn or steam "dummy" trolleys **(2)** ran between Newburyport and Amesbury (formerly Salisbury), Massachusetts, before 1890. The first electric trolley car came to Burlington, Vermont, in 1891 **(3)**.

(1)

(2)

First Electric Trolly car. 1891 Burlington, Vt.

(3)

Busy Fingers

FOUR "FIRSTS"

The old chain suspension bridge over the Merrimac River. It was known as the "Oldest Suspension Bridge in America" at the time of its replacement.

The world's first (1887) Roller Coaster— or Roller Toboggan as it was first called. Built by Stephen Jackson of Newburyport, it was the forerunner of those at Coney Island, Canobie Lake, and other amusement parks.

Henry Glover's wind-powered tool mill at W. Dedham, Mass. in 1890—the only tool mill in Norfolk County (perhaps in all of Massachusetts) so powered.

John Poyen's Atlantic Dory Shop on Carriage Hill, Amesbury, Massachusetts —the first attempt at a boat "assembly line." Thirty-foot Atlantic Power Dories were produced here with 2-cycle 3-part engines.

Not *all* children walked to school in the old days

All aboard for the bus downtown. . .

■ During the 1885-1912 period, a major attraction at most New England County Fairs was exhibition ballooning. A canvas balloon was filled with hot air, a circus acrobat ascended, performed, and floated to earth by parachute. This seems to be the only picture series in existence of a balloon ascension (of that period) from beginning to end. It took place in Southport, Conn. in 1904. The first photo shows the balloon being filled with hot air in a corner of the Pequot School grounds. Waiting to go up with it is Clarence C. Bonnette of St. Johnsbury, Vermont, who was to become New England's most famous and beloved balloonist. The furnace which (*continued below*)

filled the balloon with hot air and smoke is not visible in this picture. It was called a pit and was constructed of brick and mortar on top of the ground. Once the fire was going, the neck of the balloon was placed over the furnace, and in 20 to 25 minutes the sphere was inflated. Wood was fed into the pit through an iron door on the side; then kerosene or gasoline was poured in to speed the filling process. All the available men and boys, usually about 50, helped to hold the balloon down. Suddenly, Bonnette would shout, "Okay, let 'er go!" Everyone would let go at once. The next photo shows Bonnette, partially obscured by smoke, off and away. The balloon usually traveled one or two miles, and there was always a following of wagons, bicycles, men, women, and children.

Rockport, Maine, looking north
from Sea Street—1901

 helping hand

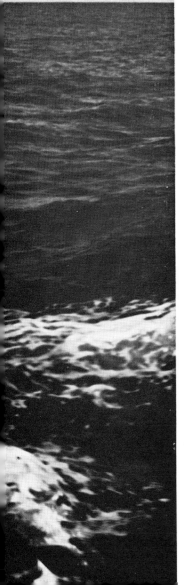

The Cross Rip Lightship—18 miles east of Woods Hole,
Massachusetts—on December 25, 1960.
She was replaced by a nine-foot lighted horn buoy
in October of 1963. All other lightships will be
or have been replaced by similar devices.

After a fishing schooner had served its time on the Grand Banks and was no longer fit for duty, she then was sold as a sand droger or granite schooner. In the last half of the 19th Century these sand drogers delivered hundreds of thousands of tons of sand to coastal cities from the beaches along the Eastern seaboard. At Plum Island Point, near Newburyport—where three drogers (above) are seen loading—a Capt. Andrew Pettengill, owner of the northern end of this point, alone sold thousands of tons on his own account.

These schooners would anchor at high tide close to shore. As the tide ebbed, they would be warped into the bank, their spars swung shoreward, and hauled over. Heavy gangplanks were then placed from hull to shore—and planks along the sand.

Schooners of 150 tons usually had a crew of three—meaning each crew member had to shovel and wheel aboard (in wheelbarrows holding half a ton)—50 tons of sand between two tides. Discharging the sand meant shovelling the cargo into dock-side buckets subsequently hoisted by horsepower onto the dock. The crew received about one dollar per ton or $50 per trip, less 15¢ to the owner of the beach, less keep, less the share to the owner of the droger—or a net of $25 per month. Sand barges later superseded the schooners—see right. In the photo at right, above, a small fishing schooner, the *I Am Here*, is tied up alongside a large granite schooner which is being loaded at Lanesville, Massachusetts with paving blocks (see piles of same behind the horse wagons) for Boston's famous streets of cobblestones.

Oliver Ingersoll, model for Winslow Homer, and Capt. Eben Davis, both of Annisquam, Mass., playing checkers. Ingersoll lived in the old schooner *Belle Gilmore* which was wharfed at the junction of River Road (then Curve St.) and Leonard St. The photo was taken prior to 1900— probably 1895— by Martha H. Harvey.

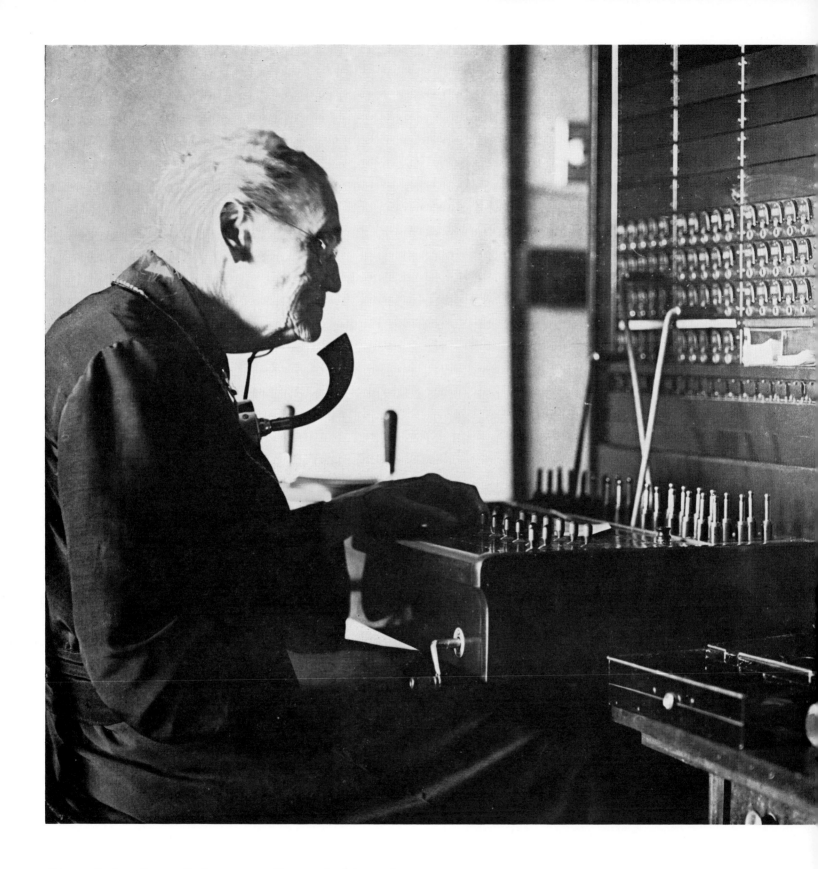

One of the first of the party-line switchboard operators, Agnes Carr of Chesterfield, N.H., just before she retired. What stories she could (but would not) have told!

Eunice Randall Thompson of Lovell, Maine, making the first radio broadcast at Medford Hillside, Massachusetts—about 1921.

Old Gloucester, Massachusetts

179

This is the Bayley Wharf (Newburyport, Massachusetts) and warehouse with molasses barrels ready to be hauled away to the warehouses of the purchasers—then to be distilled for rum. The date is probably in the 1870s. One of the firm's big schooners has just arrived and the hogsheads of molasses and sugar are being unloaded. A mare named Bess is hitched to a chaise in the foreground. This horse ran away on one occasion and, heading down the wharf, went aboard the firm's schooner *Edward Lameyer* and fell down the after hatch. Later, she was hoisted out of the main hatch—not much the worse for her fall but the chaise wasn't much good. Another light wagon is at the right—also a jiffey or low-platformed vehicle upon which the hogsheads were hauled away to the warehouses of the purchasers. The men with the high silk hats were undoubtly members of the firm. The "taster," who sampled the hogsheads to determine the quality of the molasses, is bending over the hogsheads at the left. The two boys are looking the hogsheads over for any sweetness that has oozed out between the staves.

This is the Castelhun cottage at Plum Island, Mass., on July 14, 1895. In the background can be seen the *Abbie and Eva Hooper* imbedded in the sand. She had gone aground on July 4th in a storm and was pulled back out to sea on the day this photo was taken. (This achievement was accomplished by the largest tug ever to come into the Merrimac River, the *Right Arm*). The photo was taken by the grandfather of Karl Castelhun, the little boy in the center.

Tremont Street, Boston, Massachusetts. Our guess: 1925.

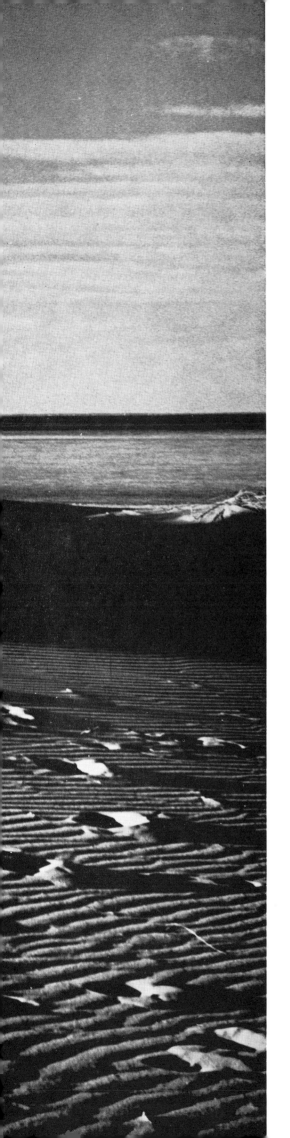

Crane's Beach, Ipswich, Massachusetts

Lives of great men all remind us
We can make our lives sublime,
And, departing, leave behind us
Footprints on the sands of time.
"A Psalm of Life"
HENRY WADSWORTH LONGFELLOW

INDEX

CREDITS

Blackington Collection: 4-5, 6-7, 8-9, 12-13, 22-23, 24-25, 28-29, 30-31, 33, 42-43, 46-47, 61, 63, 71, 74-75, 76, 78, 83, 98-99, 102-3, 112-3, 120-1, 123, 128-9, 136-7, 138, 142, 143, 144, 148, 154-5, 162, 176-7, 186-7; *Emile D. Beauchesne:* 10-11; *Fred S. Howard:* 14-15, 50-51; *Oak Ridge Portrait Studio:* 15; *Robert W. Miller Collection:* 15; *John H. Harris:* 16-17; *E. A. McDuffee:* 18-19; *Steamship Historical Society of America:* 21, 78-9, 100-1, 104-5, 144, 146, 150-1, 156-7, 160-1, 172, 180-1; *Cheney Collection:* 34-9, 64-5, 77; *Maritime History of the Merrimac:* 34-9, 64-5; *George Noyes Collection:* 34; *Frank E. Claes:* 38-9, 132-3, 166-7; *George French:* 40-1, 66-7, 96-7, 124-5, 168-9; *R. B. Hoit:* 48-9, 80-1, 122, 157; *Goodspeed Collection:* 50, 118-9, 134-5, 140-1, 152-3; *Robb Sagendorph:* 51, 55, 84-5; *Rachael Anderson:* 53; *Richard Estes:* 54; *H. D. Allison:* 54, 106-7; *Arthur W. Nelson:* 54; *Robert P. Emrick:* 56-7; *New Haven Colony Historical Society, courtesy T. S. Bronson:* 58-9, 60-1, 68-9, 86-7, 114, 130-1; *Frances Cook Macgregor:* 60-1; *This Is America:* 60-1; *E. D. Putnam:* 62, 144, 145, 146, 147; *H. S. Winslow:* 63; *L. F. Willard:* 70, 170-1; *H. E. Hammond:* 72-3; *Walter G. Cady:* 82, 132-3, 138; *Harry Packard:* 82, 116-7, 145; *George Brayton:* 88; *Aubrey Janion:* 90-93; *Eleanor Hutchinson:* 94-5; *Martha Harvey Collection (courtesy Elliott Rogers):* 108-9, 173, 174-5; *Edith LaFrancis:* 110-11; *Rev. Wm. J. Ballou:* 106-7, 133, 158-9; *Charles Hiram Thayer:* 120; *Ralph M. Arnold:* 126-7; *Chester Howland:* 135; *Stella Drury:* 142, 146; *U. Stephen Johnson:* 143; *Edward Blake:* 163; *Connecticut Aeronautical Historical Association:* 164-5; *Eva M. Gardner:* 178-9; *Castelhun Collection:* 184-5; *Hans Wendler:* 188-9.